POEMS TO
SWIPE RIGHT TO

POEMS TO SWIPE RIGHT TO

Edited and introduced by
CHARLIE CASTELLETTI

MACMILLAN COLLECTOR'S LIBRARY

This collection first published 2024 by Macmillan Collector's Library
an imprint of Pan Macmillan
The Smithson, 6 Briset Street, London EC1M 5NR
EU representative: Macmillan Publishers Ireland Ltd, 1st Floor,
The Liffey Trust Centre, 117–126 Sheriff Street Upper,
Dublin 1, DO1 YC43
Associated companies throughout the world
www.panmacmillan.com

ISBN 978-1-0350-2049-2

Selection and introduction © Charlie Castelletti 2024

The permissions acknowledgements on pp. 221–3 constitute
an extension of this copyright page.

1 3 5 7 9 8 6 4 2

A CIP catalogue record for this book is available from the British Library.

Cover and endpaper design: Daisy Bates, Pan Macmillan Art Department
Typeset in Plantin by Jouve (UK), Milton Keynes
Printed and bound in China by Imago

Visit **www.panmacmillan.com** to read more
about all our books and to buy them.

Contents

CONTENT, HAPPY IN BEING TOGETHER,
SPEAKING LITTLE,
PERHAPS NOT A WORD

#TRIALRUN #DATING

WITH ARMS, LEGS, LIPS CLOSE
CLINGING TO EMBRACE,
SHE CLIPS ME TO HER BREAST,
AND SUCKS ME TO HER FACE

#NETFLIXANDCHILL

WHEN YOUR LOVE BEGINS TO WANE, SPARE ME FROM THE CRUEL PAIN

#INTERESTLOST

THEE, EVER-PRESENT, PHANTOM THING

#GHOSTED

FAREWELL TO THEE,
BUT NOT FAREWELL

#BREAKUP

AND WE'LL LIVE OUR
WHOLE YOUNG LIVES AWAY
IN THE JOYS OF A LIVING LOVE

#YOUANDI4EVA

I SO LIKED YOU

#THEONETHATGOTAWAY
#STILLITHINKOFYOU

I LONGED FOR YOU WITH YOUR
MANTLE OF LOVE TO FOLD ME
OVER, AND DRIVE FROM OUT OF
MY BODY THE DEEP COLD THAT
HAD SUNK TO MY SOUL, AND THERE
KEPT HOLD

#CUFFINGSEASON

ARE YOU LOVING ENOUGH?

#ADVICE

Introduction
Charlie Castelletti

Most of us will have experienced the motion of swiping for love at least once in our lives – either through our own online dating adventures or by witnessing the highs and lows of our best friend's or divorced aunt's app-based dating antics. There is much excitement to be had both as participant and as bystander; you've got the set-up of the profile, the enjoyment of reading and discovering your potential interest's short but snappy bios, or the sheer revelling in their answers to *those* five questions, which hopefully promise a mix of wit and intelligence. But, more often than not, we'll get a real glimpse into their personalities through the dreaded lines: 'sorted guy looking for fun', 'let's grab a drink and see what happens' or, my personal favourite, 'here for a good time not a long time'.

Based on these snippets, we have the titillating decision-based swipe to make. Will they match with you? Of course they will, you're a catch! And if they don't, well, clearly they're too shallow and that's on *them*. Or, it might not be love that you're looking for after all – there is much more to online dating than settling down with 'the one', and a little Netflix and chill never hurt anyone . . . right? Don't quote me on that.

Eventually you'll meet your match and book that nerve-wracking first date, which could go extremely well but could also go very, very wrong. Have you ever had someone do any of the following?

1) Not show up.
2) Show up and have you wishing they hadn't.
3) Show up looking like a completely different person to their profile pic.
4) Show up and bore you to death.
5) Show up and say something cringe.
6) Show up and, what do you know? It went well . . . only for them to ghost you when you get home and disappear from the face of the earth.

I'm sure you have, and it's completely rational that some of us begrudge the very modern notion of online dating – *where is the chivalry, the romance? I just want to meet someone the 'normal' way, in a bar somewhere on a Friday night while drinking a pink gin and lemonade with my friends. Is that too much to ask for?* Apparently so. But how much has really changed when it comes to wooing?

In this anthology, I use classical poetry to show that the feelings and experiences related to online dating are not all that unique or modern, but an emotional journey that humans have been experiencing for years. For so many years, in fact, that if you strip out the 'online' part of this voyage, much of the feelings and experiences remain true to those who've come before us. From poetry drawn from the past through the likes of Emily Dickinson, Marcel Proust, Thomas Hardy, Ella Wheeler Wilcox, A. E. Housman and many more, you'll see that while the technology or language might have shifted, the desire to find one's match has never really changed, and today's methods of wooing have more in common with our ancestors than we might think.

Poems to Swipe Right to takes you through the steps and routes of modern dating rituals in ten sections. We begin with the initial selection, the tapping and swiping; the analysing of the profile; the writing of the first message – don't be generic, but don't be shallow. Don't be coy, but don't be forward, either. Will the conversation flow, or end before it even begins? The second section is all about the meet-up. The first date. A trial run. Who knows how things might turn out . . . For those lucky enough to progress to the next level, the third section, with its enticing title *'with arms, legs, lips close clinging to embrace, she clips me to her breast, and sucks me to her face'* offers up the sexy realm of 'Netflix and chill'. You all know what that means. Sections four and five are for when things turn a little sour: *'when your love begins to wane, spare me from the cruel pain'* explores the waning interest in your situationship, while *'thee, ever-present, phantom thing'* highlights the very real feelings evoked from the crime that we've all committed or been victim to at least once: ghosting. Section six relates to the inevitable break-up and the realisation that not all things can last. Section seven, however, is for those lucky enough to stay together for the long haul, or strong enough to endure their significant other for better and for worse. By contrast, eight is for the one we'll never forget, the one we wish we could do everything over for – the one who got away. Section nine is for the cold and lonely winter months, for those who seek comfort in something they know will not last but, for the moment, warmth and cuddles are what's needed. That's right, it's cuffing season. The final section is for those who could use some important advice from those who've been through it all before, invoking one simple question that we might ask ourselves as we wade through the rest of our lives: 'Are you loving enough?'

POEMS TO
SWIPE RIGHT TO

I FIND THIS FRENZY INSUFFICIENT
REASON FOR CONVERSATION

#SWIPELEFTSWIPERIGHT

Going to Him! Happy letter!

Going to Him! Happy letter!
Tell Him –
Tell Him the page I did'nt write –
Tell Him – I only said the Syntax –
And left the Verb and the pronoun – out –
Tell Him just how the fingers hurried –
Then – how they waded – slow – slow –
And then you wished you had eyes in your
   pages –
So you could see what moved them so –

Tell Him – it was'nt a Practised Writer –
You guessed – from the way the sentence
   toiled –
You could hear the Boddice tug, behind you –
As if it held but the might of a child –
You almost pitied it – you – it worked so –
Tell Him – No – you may quibble there –
For it would split His Heart, to know it –
And then you and I, were silenter.

Tell Him – Night finished – before we
    finished –
And the Old Clock kept neighing 'Day'!
And you – got sleepy –
And begged to be ended –
What would it hinder so – to – say?
Tell Him – just how she sealed you – Cautious!
But – if He ask where you are hid
Until tomorrow – Happy letter!
Gesture Coquette – and shake your Head!

Emily Dickinson

Happy Letter

Fly, little note,
And know no rest
Till warm you lie
Within that nest
Which is her breast;
Though why to thee
Such joy should be
Who carest not,
While I must wait
Here desolate,
I cannot wot.
O what I'd do
To come with you!

Richard Le Gallienne

Invitation to Love

Come when the nights are bright with stars
    Or when the moon is mellow;
Come when the sun his golden bars
    Drops on the hay-field yellow.
Come in the twilight soft and gray,
Come in the night or come in the day,
Come, O love, whene'er you may,
    And you are welcome, welcome.

You are sweet, O Love, dear Love,
You are soft as the nesting dove.
Come to my heart and bring it rest
As the bird flies home to its welcome nest.

Come when my heart is full of grief
    Or when my heart is merry;
Come with the falling of the leaf
    Or with the redd'ning cherry.
Come when the year's first blossom blows,
Come when the summer gleams and glows,
Come with the winter's drifting snows,
    And you are welcome, welcome.

Paul Laurence Dunbar

Essay to Miss Catharine Jay

An S A now I mean 2 write
    2 U sweet K T J,
The girl without a ||,
    The belle of U T K.

I 1 der if U got that 1
    I wrote 2 U B 4
I sailed in the R K D A,
    And sent by L N Moore.

My M T head will scarce contain
    A calm I D A bright
But A T miles from U I must
    M ~ this chance 2 write.

And 1st, should N E N V U,
    B E Z, mind it not,
Should N E friendship show, B true:
    They should not B forgot.

From virt U nev R D V 8;
 Her influence B 9
A like induces 10 dern S,
 Or 40 tude D vine.

And if U cannot cut a——
 Or cut an!
I hope U'll put a.
 2 I ?.

R U for an X ation 2,
 My cous N?—heart and ☞
He off R's in a ¶
 A § 2 of land.

He says he loves U 2 X S,
 U R virtuous and Y's,
In X L N C U X L
 All others in his i's.

This S A, until U I C,
 I pray U 2 X Q's,
And do not burn in F E G
 My young and wayward muse.

Now fare U well, dear K T J,
    I trust that U R true—
When this U C, then you can say,
    An S A I O U.

Charles Bombaugh

Female Fashions for 1799

A form as any taper, fine;
    A head like half-pint bason;
Where golden cords, and bands entwine,
    As rich as fleece of Jason.

A pair of shoulders strong and wide,
    Like country clown enlisting;
Bare arms long dangling by the side,
    And shoes of ragged listing!

Cravats like towels, thick and broad,
    Long tippets made of bear-skin,
Muffs that a Russian might applaud,
    And rouge to spoil a fair skin.

Long petticoats to hide the feet,
    Silk hose with clocks of scarlet;
A load of perfume, sickening sweet,
    Bought of Parisian varlet.

A bush of hair, the brow to shade,
    Sometimes the eyes to cover;

A necklace that might be display'd
    By Otaheitean lover!

A bowl of straw to deck the head,
    Like porringer unmeaning;
A bunch of puppies flaming red,
    With motley ribands streaming.

Bare ears on either side the head,
    Like wood-wild savage satyr;
Tinted with deep vermillion red,
    To shame the blush of nature.

Red elbows, gauzy gloves, that add
    An icy covering merely;
A wadded coat, the shape to pad,
    Like Dutch women—or nearly.

Such is caprice! but, lovely kind!
    Oh! let each mental feature
Proclaim the labour of the mind,
    And leave your charms to nature.

Mary Robinson

Male Fashions for 1799

Faces painted pink and brown;
    Waistcoats stripp'd and gaudy;
Sleeves thrice doubled thick with down,
    And straps to brace the body.

Short great-coats that reach the knees,
    Boots like French postillion;
Worn the G——race to please,
    But laugh'd at by the million.

Square-toed shoes, with silken strings,
    Pantaloons not fitting;
Finger deck'd with wedding rings,
    And small-clothes made of knitting.

Bull-dogs grim, and boxers bold,
    In noble trains attending;
Science which is bought with gold,
    And flatterers vice commending.

Hair cords, and plain rings, to show
　　Many a lady's favour,
Bought by every vaunting beau,
　　With mischievous endeavour.

Such is giddy Fashion's son!
　　Such a modern lover!
Oh! would their reign had ne'er begun!
　　And may it soon be over!

Mary Robinson

Madame, it's possible that
I have forgotten

Madame, it's possible that I have forgotten
Your divine and birdlike profile,
That I have pushed past my own madness
Like one jumping through a hoop,
But always still your eyes will shine
Like bright chandeliers on the ceiling of my
  mind.

Marcel Proust

I'm Nobody! Who are you?

I'm Nobody! Who are you?
Are you – Nobody – Too?
Then there's a pair of us!
Don't tell! they'd advertise – you know!

How dreary – to be – Somebody!
How public – like a Frog –
To tell one's name – the livelong June –
To an admiring Bog!

Emily Dickinson

Modern Love: V

A message from her set his brain aflame.
A world of household matters filled her mind,
Wherein he saw hypocrisy designed:
She treated him as something that is tame,
And but at other provocation bites.
Familiar was her shoulder in the glass,
Through that dark rain: yet it may come to
    pass
That a changed eye finds such familiar sights
More keenly tempting than new loveliness.
The 'What has been' a moment seemed his
    own:
The splendours, mysteries, dearer because
    known,
Nor less divine: Love's inmost sacredness,
Called to him, 'Come!'–In his restraining
    start,
Eyes nurtured to be looked at, scarce could
    see
A wave of the great waves of Destiny
Convulsed at a checked impulse of the heart.

George Meredith

To a Stranger

Passing stranger! you do not know how
 longingly I look upon you,
You must be he I was seeking, or she I was
 seeking, (it comes to me as of a dream,)
I have somewhere surely lived a life of joy with
 you,
All is recall'd as we flit by each other, fluid,
 affectionate, chaste, matured,
You grew up with me, were a boy with me or a
 girl with me,
I ate with you and slept with you, your body
 has become not yours only nor left my body
 mine only,
You give me the pleasure of your eyes, face,
 flesh, as we pass, you take of my beard,
 breast, hands, in return,
I am not to speak to you, I am to think of you
 when I sit alone or wake at night alone,
I am to wait, I do not doubt I am to meet you
 again,
I am to see to it that I do not lose you.

Walt Whitman

You're young, you've hooked me

You're young. You've hooked me. I'm the fish
you have caught. Pull me where you want
to—but don't run, you might lose me.

Strato

Oh, Is It Love?

O is it Love or is it Fame,
    This thing for which I sigh?
Or has it then no earthly name
    For men to call it by?

I know not what can ease my pains,
    Nor what it is I wish;
The passion at my heart-strings strains
    Like a tiger in a leash.

Amy Levy

The Defiance

By Heaven 'tis false, I am not vain;
    And rather would the subject be
Of your indifference, or disdain,
    Than wit or raillery.

Take back the trifling praise you give,
    And pass it on some other fool,
Who may the injuring wit believe,
    That turns her into ridicule.

Tell her, she's witty, fair, and gay,
    With all the charms that can subdue:
Perhaps she'll credit what you say;
    But curse me if I do.

If your diversion you design,
    On my good-nature you have prest:
Or if you do intend it mine,
    You have mistook the jest.

Aphra Ben

Scientific Wooing

I was a youth of studious mind,
Fair Science was my mistress kind,
    And held me with attraction chemic;
No germs of Love attacked my heart,
Secured as by Pasteurian art
    Against that fatal epidemic.

For when my daily task was o'er
I dreamed of H_2SO_4,
    Whilst stealing through my slumbers
      placid
Came Iodine, with violet fumes,
And Sulphur, with its yellow blooms,
    And whiffs of Hydrochloric Acid.

My daily visions, thoughts, and schemes
With wildest hope illumed my dreams,
    The daring dreams of trustful twenty:
I might accomplish my desire,
And set the river Thames on fire
    If but Potassium were in plenty!

Alas! that yearnings so sublime
Should all be blasted in their prime
    By hazel eyes and lips vermilion!
Ye gods! restore the halcyon days
While yet I walked in Wisdom's ways,
    And knew not Mary Maud Trevylyan!

Yet nay! the sacrilegious prayer
Was not mine own, oh fairest fair!
    Thee, dear one, will I ever cherish;
Thy worshipped image small remain
In the grey thought-cells of my brain
    Until their form and function perish.

Away with books, away with cram
For Intermediate Exam.!
    Away with every college duty!
Though once Agnostic to the core,
A virgin Saint I now adore,
    And swear belief in Love and Beauty.

Yet when I meet her tranquil gaze,
I dare not plead, I dare not praise,
    Like other men with other lasses;

She's never kind, she's never coy,
She treats me simply as a boy,
    And asks me how I like my classes!

I covet not her golden dower –
Yet surely Love's attractive power
    Directly as the mass must vary –
But ah! inversely as the square
Of distance! shall I ever dare
    To cross the gulf, and gain my Mary?

So chill she seems – and yet she might
Welcome with radiant heat and light
    My courtship, if I once began it;
For is not e'en the palest star
That gleams so coldly from afar
    A sun to some revolving planet?

My Mary! be a solar sphere!
Envy no comet's mad career,
    No arid, airless lunar crescent!
Oh for a spectroscope to show
That in thy gentle eyes doth glow
    Love's vapour, pure and incandescent!

Bright fancy! can I fail to please
If with similitudes like these
    I lure the maid to sweet communion?
My suit, with Optics well begun,
By Magnetism shall be won,
      And closed at last in Chemic union!

At this I'll aim, for this I'll toil,
And this I'll reach – I will, by Boyle,
    By Avogadro, and by Davy!
When every science lends a trope
To feed my love, to fire my hope,
      Her maiden pride must cry '*Peccavi!*'

I'll sing a deep Darwinian lay
Of little birds with plumage gay,
    Who solved by courtship Life's enigma;
I'll teach her how the wild-flowers love,
And why the trembling stamens move,
      And how the anthers kiss the stigma.

  Or Mathematically true
  With rigorous Logic will I woo,
     And not a word I'll say at random;

Till urged by Syllogistic stress,
She falter forth a tearful 'Yes,'
    A sweet '*Quod erat demonstrandum!*'

Constance Naden

Somewhere or Other

Somewhere or other there must surely be
 The face not seen, the voice not heard,
The heart that not yet—never yet—ah me!
 Made answer to my word.

Somewhere or other, may be near or far;
 Past land and sea, clean out of sight;
Beyond the wandering moon, beyond the star
 That tracks her night by night.

Somewhere or other, may be far or near;
 With just a wall, a hedge, between;
With just the last leaves of the dying year
 Fallen on a turf grown green.

Christina Rossetti

Ships That Pass in the Night

Out in the sky the great dark clouds are
    massing;
      I look far out into the pregnant night,
Where I can hear a solemn booming gun
      And catch the gleaming of a random light,
That tells me that the ship I seek is passing,
    passing.

My tearful eyes my soul's deep hurt are
    glassing;
      For I would hail and check that ship of
        ships.
I stretch my hands imploring, cry aloud,
      My voice falls dead a foot from mine own
        lips,
And but its ghost doth reach that vessel,
    passing, passing.

O Earth, O Sky, O Ocean, both surpassing,
      O heart of mine, O soul that dreads the
        dark!
Is there no hope for me? Is there no way

That I may sight and check that speeding
   bark
Which out of sight and sound is passing,
   passing?

Paul Laurence Dunbar

Since you always keep these
notes diverse

Since you always keep these notes diverse.
I am obliged to write in verse,
If you don't feel list-
Less, Nicolas the nationalist,
In twenty minutes give me,
A nice, steamy, milky coffee.

Marcel Proust

Two Young Men, 23 to 24 Years Old

He'd been sitting in the café since ten-thirty
expecting him to turn up any minute.
Midnight had gone, and he was still waiting
    for him.
It was now after one-thirty, and the café was
    almost deserted.
He'd grown tired of reading newspapers
mechanically. Of his three lonely shillings
only one was left: waiting that long,
he'd spent the others on coffees and brandy.
And he'd smoked all his cigarettes.
So much waiting had worn him out.
Because alone like that for so many hours,
he'd also begun to have disturbing thoughts
about the immoral life he was living.

But when he saw his friend come in—
weariness, boredom, thought all disappeared
    at once.

His friend brought unexpected news.
He'd won sixty pounds playing cards.

Their good looks, their exquisite youthfulness,
the sensitive love they shared
were refreshed, livened, invigorated
by the sixty pounds from the card table.

Now all joy and vitality, feeling and charm,
they went—not to the homes of their
    respectable families
(where they were no longer wanted anyway)—
they went to a familiar and very special
house of debauchery, and they asked for a
    bedroom
and expensive drinks, and they drank again.

And when the expensive drinks were finished
and it was close to four in the morning,
happy, they gave themselves to love.

Constantine P. Cavafy

CONTENT, HAPPY IN BEING
TOGETHER, SPEAKING LITTLE,
PERHAPS NOT A WORD

#TRIALRUN #DATING

I, being born a woman and distressed

I, being born a woman and distressed
By all the needs and notions of my kind,
Am urged by your propinquity to find
Your person fair, and feel a certain zest
To bear your body's weight upon my breast:
So subtly is the fume of life designed,
To clarify the pulse and cloud the mind,
And leave me once again undone, possessed.
Think not for this, however, the poor treason
Of my stout blood against my staggering
  brain,
I shall remember you with love, or season
My scorn with pity,–let me make it plain:
I find this frenzy insufficient reason
For conversation when we meet again.

Edna St. Vincent Millay

Nerves

The modern malady of love is nerves.
Love, once a simple madness, now observes
The stages of his passionate disease,
And is twice sorrowful because he sees,
Inch by inch entering, the fatal knife.
O health of simple minds, give me your life,
And let me, for one midnight, cease to hear
The clock for ever ticking in my ear,
The clock that tells the minutes in my brain.
It is not love, nor love's despair, this pain
That shoots a witless, keener pang across
The simple agony of love and loss.
Nerves, nerves! O folly of a child who dreams
Of heaven, and, waking in the darkness,
  screams.

Arthur Symons

A Glimpse

A glimpse through an interstice caught,
Of a crowd of workmen and drivers in a
  bar-room
    around the stove late of a winter night,
      and I
    unremark'd seated in a corner,
Of a youth who loves me and whom I love,
  silently
    approaching and seating himself near, that
      he may
    hold me by the hand,
A long while amid the noises of coming and
  going,
    of drinking and oath and smutty jest,
There we two, content, happy in being
  together,
    speaking little, perhaps not a word.

Walt Whitman

A Drinking Song

Wine comes in at the mouth
And love comes in at the eye;
That's all we shall know for truth
Before we grow old and die.
I lift the glass to my mouth,
I look at you, and I sigh.

W. B. Yeats

A Glass of Wine

"What's in a glass of wine?"
    There, set the glass where I can look
      within.
Now listen to me, friend, while I begin
    And tell you what I see–
What I behold with my far-reaching eyes,
    And what I know to be
Below the laughing bubbles that arise
    Within this glass of wine.
There is a little spirit, night and day,
That cries one word, for ever and alway:
    That single word is "More!"
And whoso drinks a glass of wine, drinks *him*:
You fill the goblet full unto the brim,
    And strive to silence him.

Glass after glass you drain to quench his
    thirst,
Each glass contains a spirit like the first;
    And all their voices cry
Until they shriek and clamor, howl and rave,
    And shout "More!" noisily,

Till welcome death prepares the drunkard's
    grave,
        And stills the imps that rave.

        That see I in the wine:
And tears so many that I cannot guess;
And all these drops are labelled with
    "Distress."
        I know you cannot see.
And at the bottom are the dregs of shame:
        Oh! it is plain to me.
And there are woes too terrible to name:
Now drink your glass of wine.

Ella Wheeler Wilcox

Anticipation

I have been temperate always,
But I am like to be very drunk
With your coming.
There have been times
I feared to walk down the street
Lest I should reel with the wine of you,
And jerk against my neighbours
As they go by.
I am parched now, and my tongue is horrible
    in my mouth,
But my brain is noisy
With the clash and gurgle of filling wine-cups.

Amy Lowell

Nocturne

One little cab to hold us two,
Night, an invisible dome of cloud,
The rattling wheels that made our whispers
    loud,
As heart-beats into whispers grew;
And, long, the Embankment with its lights,
The pavement glittering with fallen rain,
The magic and mystery that is night's,
And human love without the pain.

The river shook with wavering gleams,
Deep buried as the glooms that lay
Impenetrable as the grave of day,
Near and as distant as our dreams.
A bright train flashed with all its squares
Of warm light where the bridge lay mistily.
The night was all about us: we were free,
Free of the day and all its cares!

That was an hour of bliss too long,
Too long to last where joy is brief.
Yet one escape of souls may yield relief
To many weary seasons' wrong.

'O last for ever!' my heart cried;
It ended: heaven was done.
I had been dreaming by her side
That heaven was but begun.

Arthur Symons

A Thunderstorm in Town

(A Reminiscence: 1893)

She wore a new 'terra-cotta' dress,
And we stayed, because of the pelting storm,
Within the hansom's dry recess,
Though the horse had stopped; yea,
   motionless
     We sat on, snug and warm.
Then the downpour ceased, to my sharp sad
   pain,
And the glass that had screened our forms
   before
Flew up, and out she sprang to her door:
I should have kissed her if the rain
     Had lasted a minute more.

Thomas Hardy

44

Love is Like a Dizziness

O, love, love, love!
Love is like a dizziness;
It winna let a puir body
Gang about his biziness!

James Hogg

To a Lady that Desired
I Would Love Her

Now you have freely given me leave to love,
What will you do?
Shall I your mirth, or passion move,
When I begin to woo;
Will you torment, or scorn, or love me too?

Each petty beauty can disdain, and I
Spite of your hate
Without your leave can see, and die;
Dispense a nobler fate!
'Tis easy to destroy, you may create.

Then give me leave to love, and love me too
Not with design
To raise, as Love's cursed rebels do,
When puling poets whine,
Fame to their beauty, from their blubbered
   eyne.

Grief is a puddle, and reflects not clear
Your beauty's rays;

Joys are pure streams, your eyes appear
Sullen in sadder lays;
In cheerful numbers they shine bright with
    praise,

Which shall not mention to express you fair,
Wounds, flames, and darts,
Storms in your brow, nets in your hair,
Suborning all your parts,
Or to betray, or torture captive hearts.

I'll make your eyes like morning suns appear,
As mild, and fair;
Your brow as crystal smooth, and clear,
And your disheveled hair
Shall flow like a calm region of the air.

                                    Thomas Carew

Simile

The little Moth round candle turning,
Stops not till its wings are burning:
So woman, dazzled by man's wooing,
Rushes to her own undoing.

Charlotte Dacre

Kisses Loathsome

I abhor the slimy kiss,
Which to me most loathsome is.
Those lips please me which are placed
Close, but not too strictly laced:
Yielding I would have them; yet
Not a wimbling tongue admit:
What should poking-sticks make there,
When the ruffe is set elswhere?

Robert Herrick

Alas, madam, for stealing of a kiss

Alas, madam, for stealing of a kiss
Have I so much your mind there offended?
Have I then done so grievously amiss
That by no means it may be amended?

Then revenge you, and the next way is this:
Another kiss shall have my life ended,
For to my mouth the first my heart did suck;
The next shall clean out of my breast it pluck.

Thomas Carew

Intimates

Don't you care for my love? she said bitterly.

I handed her the mirror, and said:
Please address these questions to the proper
    person!
Please make all requests to head-quarters!
In all matters of emotional importance
please approach the supreme authority
    direct! –
So I handed her the mirror.

And she would have broken it over my head,
but she caught sight of her own reflection
and that held her spellbound for two seconds
while I fled.

D. H. Lawrence

Because I liked you better

Because I liked you better
　　Than suits a man to say,
It irked you, and I promised
　　To throw the thought away.

To put the world between us
　　We parted, stiff and dry;
'Good-bye,' said you, 'forget me.'
　　'I will, no fear,' said I.

If here, where clover whitens
　　The dead man's knoll, you pass,
And no tall flower to meet you
　　Starts in the trefoiled grass,

Halt by the headstone naming
　　The heart no longer stirred,
And say the lad that loved you
　　Was one that kept his word.

A. E. Housman

Whoever you are holding me now in hand

Whoever you are holding me now in hand,
Without one thing all will be useless,
I give you fair warning before you attempt me
    further,
I am not what you supposed, but far different.

Who is he that would become my follower?
Who would sign himself a candidate for my
    affections?

The way is suspicious, the result uncertain,
    perhaps destructive,
You would have to give up all else, I alone
    would expect to be your sole and exclusive
    standard,
Your novitiate would even then be long and
    exhausting,
The whole past theory of your life and all
    conformity to the lives around you would
    have to be abandon'd,

Therefore release me now before troubling
    yourself any further, let go your hand from
    my shoulders,
Put me down and depart on your way.

Or else by stealth in some wood for trial,
Or back of a rock in the open air,
(For in any roof'd room of a house I emerge
    not, nor in company,
And in libraries I lie as one dumb, a gawk, or
    unborn, or dead,)
But just possibly with you on a high hill, first
    watching lest any person for miles around
    approach unawares,
Or possibly with you sailing at sea, or on the
    beach of the sea or some quiet island,
Here to put your lips upon mine I permit you,
With the comrade's long-dwelling kiss or the
    new husband's kiss,
For I am the new husband and I am the
    comrade.

Or if you will, thrusting me beneath your
    clothing,

Where I may feel the throbs of your heart or
    rest upon your hip,
Carry me when you go forth over land or sea;
For thus merely touching you is enough, is
    best,
And thus touching you would I silently sleep
    and be carried eternally.

But these leaves conning you con at peril,
For these leaves and me you will not
    understand,
They will elude you at first and still more
    afterward, I will certainly elude you,
Even while you should think you had
    unquestionably caught me, behold!
Already you see I have escaped from you.

For it is not for what I have put into it that I
    have written this book,
Nor is it by reading it you will acquire it,
Nor do those know me best who admire me
    and vauntingly praise me,
Nor will the candidates for my love (unless at
    most a very few) prove victorious,

Nor will my poems do good only, they will do
  just as much evil, perhaps more,
For all is useless without that which you may
  guess at many times and not hit, that which
  I hinted at;
Therefore release me and depart on your way.

Walt Whitman

The Female Philosopher

You tell me, fair one, that you ne'er can love,
And seem with scorn to mock the dangerous
  fire;
But why, then, trait'ress, do you seek to move
In others what your breast can ne'er inspire?

You tell me, you my friend alone will be,
Yet speak of friendship in a voice so sweet,
That, while I struggle to be coldly free,
I feel my heart with wildest throbbings beat.

Vainly indiff'rence would you bid us feel,
While so much languor in those eyes appear;
Vainly the stoic's happiness reveal,
While soft emotion all your features wear.

O, form'd for love! O, wherefore should
  you fly
From the seducing charm it spreads around?
O why enshrine your soul with apathy?
Or wish in frozen fetters to be bound?

Life is a darksome and a dreary day,
The solitary wretch no pleasure knows;
Love is the star that lights him on his way,
And guides him on to pleasure and repose.

But oft, forgetful of thy plan severe,
I've seen thee fondly gaze—I've heard thee
　　sigh;
I've mark'd thy strain of converse, sadly dear,
While softest rapture lighten'd from thine eye.

Then have I thought some wayward youth
　　employ'd
Thy secret soul, but left thee to despair,
And oft with pleasing sorrow have enjoy'd
The task of chasing thy corrosive care.

Yet pride must save me from a dastard love,
A grov'ling love, that cannot hope return:
A soul like mine was never form'd to prove
Those viler passions with which some can
　　burn.

Then fear not me; for since it is thy will,
Adhere with stubborn coolness to thy vow;
Grant me thy philosophic friendship still—
I'll grant thee mine with all the powers I
 know.

Charlotte Dacre

WITH ARMS, LEGS, LIPS CLOSE
CLINGING TO EMBRACE,
SHE CLIPS ME TO HER BREAST,
AND SUCKS ME TO HER FACE.

#NETFLIXANDCHILL

Isabel

In her body's perfect sweet
Suppleness and languor meet,—
Arms that move like lapsing billows,
Breasts that Love would make his pillows.
Eyes where vision melts in bliss,
Lips that ripen to a kiss.

Bliss Carmen

from Fragments

★

Her skirt lifted as a dark mist
From the columns of amethyst.

★

This to all ladies gay I say.
Away, abhorréd lace, away.

★

The lark crawls on the cloud
Like a flea on a white body.

★

With a courtly bow the bent tree sighed,
May I present you to my friend the sun.

T. E. Hulme

Upon Julia's breasts

Display thy breasts, my *Julia*, there let me
Behold that circummortall purity:
Betweene whose glories; there my lips He lay,
Ravisht, in that faire *Via Lactea*.

Robert Herrick

To his Mistress Going to Bed

Come, Madam, come, all rest my powers
    defie,
Until I labour, I in labour lie.
The foe oft-times having the foe in sight,
Is tir'd with standing though he never fight.
Off with that girdle, like heavens Zone
    glittering,
But a fair fairer world incompassing.
Unpin that spangled breastplate which you
    wear,
That th'eyes of busie fooles may be stopt there.
Unlace your self, for that harmonious chyme,
Tells me from you, that now it is bed time.
Off with that happy busk, which I envie,
That still can be, and still can stand so nigh.
Your gown going off, such beautious state
    reveals,
As when from flowry meads th'hills shadowe
    steales.
Off with that wyerie Coronet and shew
The haiery Diademe which on you doth grow:
Now off with those shooes, and then softly
    tread

In this loves hallow'd temple, this soft bed.
In such white robes, heaven's Angels us'd to be
Receavd by men: thou Angel bringst with
    thee
A heaven like Mahomets Paradice, and though
Ill spirits walk in white, we easily know,
By this these Angels from an evil sprite,
Those set our hairs, but these our flesh
    upright.
        Licence my roaving hands, and let
            them go,
Before, behind, between, above, below.
O my America! my new-found-land,
My kingdome, safeliest when with one man
    man'd,
My Myne of precious stones; My Emperie,
How blest am I in this discovering thee!
To enter in these bonds, is to be free;
Then where my hand is set, my seal shall be.
        Full nakedness! All joyes are due to thee,
As souls unbodied, bodies uncloth'd must be,
To taste whole joyes. Jems which you
    women use
Are like Atlanta's balls, cast in mens views,
That when a fools eye lighteth on a Jem,

His earthly soul may covet theirs, not them:
Like pictures, or like books gay coverings
   made
For lay-men, are all women thus array'd.
Themselves are mystick books, which only wee
(Whom their imputed grace will dignifie)
Must see reveal'd. Then since that I may
   know;
As liberally, as to a Midwife shew
Thy self: cast all, yea, this white lynnen hence,
There is no pennance, much less innocence:

    To teach thee, I am naked first; why then
What needst thou have more covering then
   a man.

John Donne

The Imperfect Enjoyment

Naked she lay, clasped in my longing arms,
I filled with love, and she all over charms;
Both equally inspired with eager fire,
Melting through kindness, flaming in desire.
With arms, legs, lips close clinging to
  embrace,
She clips me to her breast, and sucks me to
  her face.
Her nimble tongue, love's lesser lightning,
  played
Within my mouth, and to my thoughts
  conveyed
Swift orders that I should prepare to throw
The all-dissolving thunderbolt below.
My fluttering soul, sprung with the pointed
  kiss,
Hangs hovering o'er her balmy brinks of bliss.
But whilst her busy hand would guide that
  part
Which should convey my soul up to her heart,
In liquid raptures I dissolve all o'er,
Melt into sperm, and spend at every pore.
A touch from any part of her had done 't:

Her hand, her foot, her very look's a cunt.
 Smiling, she chides in a kind murmuring
  noise,
And from her body wipes the clammy joys,
When, with a thousand kisses wandering o'er
My panting bosom, "Is there then no more?"
She cries. "All this to love and rapture's due;
Must we not pay a debt to pleasure too?"
 But I, the most forlorn, lost man alive,
To show my wished obedience vainly strive:
I sigh, alas! and kiss, but cannot swive.
Eager desires confound my first intent,
Succeeding shame does more success prevent,
And rage at last confirms me impotent.
Ev'n her fair hand, which might bid heat
 return
To frozen age, and make cold hermits burn,
Applied to my dear cinder, warms no more
Than fire to ashes could past flames restore.
Trembling, confused, despairing, limber, dry,
A wishing, weak, unmoving lump I lie.
This dart of love, whose piercing point, oft
 tried,
With virgin blood ten thousand maids has
 dyed,

69

Which nature still directed with such art
That it through every cunt reached every
  heart—
Stiffly resolved, 'twould carelessly invade
Woman or man, nor ought its fury stayed:
Where'er it pierced, a cunt it found or made—
Now languid lies in this unhappy hour,
Shrunk up and sapless like a withered flower.

    Thou treacherous, base deserter of my
        flame,
False to my passion, fatal to my fame,
Through what mistaken magic dost thou prove
So true to lewdness, so untrue to love?
What oyster-cinder-beggar-common whore
Didst thou e'er fail in all thy life before?
When vice, disease, and scandal lead the way,
With what officious haste doest thou obey!
Like a rude, roaring hector in the streets
Who scuffles, cuffs, and justles all he meets,
But if his king or country claim his aid,
The rakehell villain shrinks and hides his
  head;
Ev'n so thy brutal valor is displayed,
Breaks every stew, does each small whore
  invade,

But when great Love the onset does
   command,
Base recreant to thy prince, thou dar'st not
   stand.
Worst part of me, and henceforth hated most,
Through all the town a common fucking post,
On whom each whore relieves her tingling
   cunt
As hogs on gates do rub themselves and grunt,
Mayst thou to ravenous chancres be a prey,
Or in consuming weepings waste away;
May strangury and stone thy days attend;
May'st thou never piss, who didst refuse to
   spend
When all my joys did on false thee depend.
     And may ten thousand abler pricks agree
     To do the wronged Corinna right for thee.

John Wilmot, Earl of Rochester

Apotheosis

Come slowly—Eden!
Lips unused to Thee—
Bashful—sip thy Jessamines—
As the fainting Bee—

Reaching late his flower,
Round her chamber hums—
Counts his nectars—
Enters—and is lost in Balms.

Emily Dickinson

Their Sex Life

One failure on
Top of another

A. R. Ammons

The Weather-Cock Points South

I put your leaves aside,
One by one;
The stiff, broad outer leaves;
The smaller ones,
Pleasant to touch, veined with purple;
The glazed inner leaves.
One by one
I parted you from your leaves,
Until you stood up like a white flower
Swaying slightly in the evening wind.

White flower,
Flower of wax, of jade, of unstreaked agate;
Flower with surfaces of ice,
With shadows faintly crimson.
Where in all the garden is there such a flower?
The stars crowd through the lilac leaves
To look at you.
The low moon brightens you with silver.

The bud is more than the calyx.
There is nothing to equal a white bud,
Of no colour, and of all,
Burnished by moonlight,
Thrust upon by a softly-swinging wind.

Amy Lowell

City of Orgies

City of orgies, walks and joys,
City whom that I have lived and sung in your
   midst will one day make you illustrious,
Not the pageants of you, not your shifting
   tableaus, your spectacles, repay me,
Not the interminable rows of your houses, nor
   the ships at the wharves,
Not the processions in the streets, nor the
   bright windows with goods in them,
Not to converse with learn'd persons, or bear
   my share in the soiree or feast;
Not those, but as I pass O Manhattan, your
   frequent and swift flash of eyes offering me
   love,
Offering response to my own – these repay
   me,
Lovers, continual lovers, only repay me.

Walt Whitman

Parting at Morning

Round the cape of a sudden came the sea,
And the sun looked over the mountain's rim:
And straight was a path of gold for him,
And the need of a world of men for me.

Robert Browning

Good God, what a night that was

Good God, what a night that was,
The bed was so soft, and how we clung,
Burning together, lying this way and that,
Our uncontrollable passions
Flowing through our mouths.
If I could only die that way,
I'd say goodbye to the business of living.

Petronius Arbiter

WHEN YOUR LOVE BEGINS TO WANE,
SPARE ME FROM THE CRUEL PAIN

#INTERESTLOST

The Mess of Love

We've made a great mess of love
since we made an ideal of it.

The moment I swear to love a woman, a
   certain woman, all my life
that moment I begin to hate her.

The moment I even say to a woman: I love
   you!—
my love dies down considerably.

The moment love is an understood thing
   between us, we are sure of it,
it's a cold egg, it isn't love any more.

Love is like a flower, it must flower and fade;
if it doesn't fade, it is not a flower,
it's either an artificial rag blossom, or an
   immortelle, for the cemetery.

The moment the mind interferes with love, or
   the will fixes on it,

or the personality assumes it as an attribute,
   or the ego takes possession of it,
it is not love any more, it's just a mess.
And we've made a great mess of love, mind-
   perverted, will-perverted, ego-perverted
   love.

D. H. Lawrence

You say you love; but with a voice

You say you love; but with a voice
Chaster than a nun's, who singeth
The soft Vespers to herself
While the chime-bell ringeth –
O love me truly!

You say you love; but with a smile
Cold as sunrise in September,
As you were Saint Cupid's nun,
And kept his weeks of Ember.
O love me truly!

You say you love – but then your lips
Coral tinted teach no blisses.
More than coral in the sea –
They never pout for kisses –
O love me truly!

You say you love; but then your hand
No soft squeeze for squeeze returneth,
It is like a statue's dead –
While mine to passion burneth –
O love me truly!

O breathe a word or two of fire!
Smile, as if those words should burn be,
Squeeze as lovers should – O kiss
And in thy heart inurn me!
O love me truly!

John Keats

Change

Changed? Yes, I will confess it—I have
    changed.
      I do not love you in the old fond way.
I am your friend still—time has not estranged
      One kindly feeling of that vanished day.

But the bright glamour which made life a
    dream,
      The rapture of that time, its sweet
        content,
Like visions of a sleeper's brain they seem—
      And yet I cannot tell you how they went.

Why do you gaze with such accusing eyes
      Upon me, dear? Is it so very strange
That hearts, like all things underneath God's
    skies,
      Should sometimes feel the influence of
        change?

The birds, the flowers, the foliage of the trees,
      The stars which seem so fixed, and so
        sublime,

Vast continents, and the eternal seas—
    All these do change, with ever-changing
        time.

The face our mirror shows us year on year
    Is not the same; our dearest aim, or need,
Our lightest thought, or feeling, hope, or fear,
    All, all the law of alternation heed.

How can we ask the human heart to stay,
    Content with fancies of Youth's earliest
        hours?
The year outgrows the violets of May,
    Although, maybe, there are no fairer
        flowers.

And life may hold no sweeter love than this,
    Which lies so cold, so voiceless, and so
        dumb.
And will I miss it, dear? Why, yes, we miss
    The violets always—till the roses come!

Ella Wheeler Wilcox

So, we'll go no more a roving

I

So, we'll go no more a roving
So late into the night,
Though the heart be still as loving.
And the moon be still as bright

II

For the sword outwears its sheath,
And the soul wears out the breast,
And the heart must pause to breathe,
And love itself have rest

III

Though the night was made for loving,
And the day returns too soon,
Yet we'll go no more a roving
By the light of the moon.

George, Lord Byron

Virginity!

Virginity you have abandoned me!
Virginity,
where have you gone?
Virginity,
I will never return to you, no,
I shall never return
to you!

Sappho

Caprice

You held a wild-flower in your finger-tips,
Idly you pressed it to indifferent lips,
Idly you tore its crimson leaves apart . . .
Alas! it was my heart.

You held a wine-cup in your finger-tips,
Lightly you raised it to indifferent lips,
Lightly you drank and flung away the
   bowl . . .
Alas! it was my soul.

Sarojini Naidu

Once We Played

Once we played at love together—
Played it smartly, if you please;
Lightly, as a windblown feather,
Did we stake a heart apiece.

Oh, it was delicious fooling!
In the hottest of the game,
Without thought of future cooling,
All too quickly burned Life's flame.

In this give-and-take of glances,
Kisses sweet as honey dews,
When we played with equal chances,
Did you win, or did I lose?

Mathilde Blind

And if I did, what then?

'And if I did, what then?
Are you aggrieved therefore?
The sea hath fish for every man,
And what would you have more?'

Thus did my mistress once
Amaze my mind with doubt;
And popped a question for the nonce,
To beat my brains about.

Whereto I thus replied:
'Each fisherman can wish
That all the seas at every tide
Were his alone to fish;

And so did I, in vain;
But since it may not be,
Let such fish there as find the gain,
And leave the loss for me.

And with such luck and loss
I will content myself,

Till tides of turning time may toss
Such fishers on the shelf.

And when they stick on sands,
That every man may see,
Then will I laugh and clap my hands,
As they do now at me.'

George Gascoigne

Ephemera

'Your eyes that once were never weary of mine
Are bowed in sorrow under pendulous lids,
Because our love is waning.'
                              And then she:
'Although our love is waning, let us stand
By the lone border of the lake once more,
Together in that hour of gentleness
When the poor tired child, Passion, falls
    asleep:
How far away the stars seem, and how far
Is our first kiss, and ah, how old my heart!'
Pensive they paced along the faded leaves,
While slowly he whose hand held hers, replied:
'Passion has often worn our wandering hearts.'

The woods were round them, and the yellow
    leaves
Fell like faint meteors in the gloom, and once
A rabbit old and lame limped down the path;
Autumn was over him: and now they stood
On the lone border of the lake once more:
Turning, he saw that she had thrust dead
    leaves

Gathered in silence, dewy as her eyes,
In bosom and hair.
       'Ah, do not mourn,' he said,
'That we are tired, for other loves await us;
Hate on and love through unrepining hours.
Before us lies eternity; our souls
Are love, and a continual farewell.'

W. B. Yeats

The Fish

Although you hide in the ebb and flow
Of the pale tide when the moon has set,
The people of coming days will know
About the casting out of my net,
And how you have leaped times out of mind
Over the little silver cords,
And think that you were hard and unkind,
And blame you with many bitter words.

W. B. Yeats

Love Will Wane

When your love begins to wane,
　　Spare me from the cruel pain
Of all speech that tells me so—
　　Spare me words, for I shall know,

By the half-averted eyes,
　　By the breast that no more sighs,
By the rapture I shall miss
　　From your strangely-altered kiss;

By the arms that still enfold
　　But have lost their clinging hold,
And, too willing, let me go
　　I shall know, love, I shall know.

Bitter will the knowledge be,
　　Bitterer than death to me.
Yet, 'twill come to me some day,
　　For it is the sad world's way.

Make no vows—vows cannot bind
　　Changing hearts or wayward mind.

Men grow weary of a bliss
    Passionate and fond as this.

Love will wane. But I shall know,
    If you do not tell me so.
Know it, tho' you smile and say,
    That you love me more each day.

Know it by the inner sight
    That forever sees aright.
Words could but increase my woe,
    And without them, I shall know.

Ella Wheeler Wilcox

from Phantasmion

He came unlook'd for, undesir'd,
A sunrise in the northern sky,
More than the brightest dawn admir'd,
To shine and then forever fly.

His love, conferr'd without a claim,
Perchance was like the fitful blaze,
Which lives to light a steadier flame,
And, while that strengthens, fast decays.

Glad fawn along the forest springing,
Gay birds that breeze-like stir the leaves,
Why hither haste, no message bringing,
To solace one that deeply grieves?

Thou star that dost the skies adorn,
So brightly heralding the day,
Bring one more welcome than the morn,
Or still in night's dark prison stay.

Sara Coleridge

THEE, EVER-PRESENT,
PHANTOM THING

#GHOSTED

Ghosts

There are ghosts in the room,
As I sit here alone, from the dark corners there
    They come out of the gloom
And they stand at my side and they lean on
  my chair.

    There's the ghost of a Hope
That lighted my days with a fanciful glow;
    In her hand is the rope
That strangled her life out. Hope was slain
  long ago.

    But her ghost comes to-night,
With its skeleton face and expressionless eyes,
    And it stands in the light
And mocks me and jeers me with sobs and
  with sighs.

    There's a ghost of a Joy,
A frail, fragile thing, and I prized it too much,
    And the hands that destroy
Clasped it close, and it died at the withering
  touch.

There's a ghost of a Love,
Born with Joy, reared with Hope, died in pain
   and unrest;
   But he towers above
All the others–this ghost: yet a ghost at the
   best.

   I am weary, and fain
Would forget all these dead; but the gibbering
   host
   Make the struggle in vain.
In each shadowy corner there lurketh a ghost.

Ella Wheeler Wilcox

Without Ceremony

It was your way, my dear,
To vanish without a word
When callers, friends, or kin
Had left, and I hastened in
To rejoin you, as I inferred.

And when you'd a mind to career
Off anywhere – say to town –
You were all on a sudden gone
Before I had thought thereon,
Or noticed your trunks were down.

So, now that you disappear
For ever in that swift style,
Your meaning seems to me
Just as it used to be:
'Good-bye is not worth while!'

Thomas Hardy

You would have understood me, had you waited

You would have understood me, had you
    waited;
       I could have loved you, dear! as well as he:
Had we not been impatient, dear! and fated
       Always to disagree.

What is the use of speech? Silence were fitter:
       Lest we should still be wishing things
          unsaid.
Though all the words we ever spake were
    bitter,
       Shall I reproach you dead?

Nay, let this earth, your portion, likewise cover
       All the old anger, setting us apart:
Always, in all, in truth was I your lover;
       Always, I held your heart.

I have met other women who were tender,
       As you were cold, dear! with a grace as
          rare.

Think you, I turned to them, or made
    surrender,
        I who had found you fair?

Had we been patient, dear! ah, had you
    waited,
        I had fought death for you, better than he:
But from the very first, dear! we were fated
        Always to disagree.

Late, late, I come to you, now death discloses
        Love that in life was not to be our part:
On your low lying mound between the roses,
        Sadly I cast my heart.

I would not waken you: nay! this is fitter;
        Death and the darkness give you unto me;
Here we who loved so, were so cold and bitter,
        Hardly can disagree.

                                        Ernest Dowson

A Snake

Sweet is the swamp with its secrets,
Until we meet a snake;
'Tis then we sigh for houses,
And our departure take
At that enthralling gallop
That only childhood knows.
A snake is summer's treason,
And guile is where it goes.

Emily Dickinson

A Serpent-Face

His face was like a snake's – wrinkled and
  loose
And withered–

Percy Shelley

Heart, we will forget him!

Heart, we will forget him!
You and I, to-night!
You may forget the warmth he gave,
I will forget the light.

When you have done, pray tell me,
That I my thoughts may dim;
Haste! lest while you're lagging,
I may remember him!

Emily Dickinson

Plead for Me

O thy bright eyes must answer now,
When Reason, with a scornful brow,
Is mocking at my overthrow;
O thy sweet tongue must plead for me
And tell why I have chosen thee!

Stern Reason is to judgment come
Arrayed in all her forms of gloom:
Wilt thou my advocate be dumb?
No, radiant angel, speak and say
Why I did cast the world away;

Why I have persevered to shun
The common paths that others run;
And on a strange road journeyed on
Heedless alike of Wealth and Power—
Of Glory's wreath and Pleasure's flower.

These once indeed seemed Beings divine,
And they perchance heard vows of mine
And saw my offerings on their shrine—
But, careless gifts are seldom prized,
And mine were worthily despised;

So with a ready heart I swore
To seek their altar-stone no more,
And gave my spirit to adore
Thee, ever present, phantom thing—
My slave, my comrade, and my King!

A slave because I rule thee still;
Incline thee to my changeful will
And make thy influence good or ill—
A comrade, for by day and night
Thou art my intimate delight—

My Darling Pain that wounds and sears
And wrings a blessing out from tears
By deadening me to real cares;
And yet, a king—though prudence well
Have taught thy subject to rebel.

And am I wrong to worship where
Faith cannot doubt nor Hope despair,
Since my own soul can grant my prayer?
Speak, God of Visions, plead for me
And tell why I have chosen thee!

Emily Brontë

What lips my lips have kissed,
and where, and why

What lips my lips have kissed, and where, and
   why,
I have forgotten, and what arms have lain
Under my head till morning; but the rain
Is full of ghosts tonight, that tap and sigh
Upon the glass and listen for reply,
And in my heart there stirs a quiet pain
For unremembered lads that not again
Will turn to me at midnight with a cry.
Thus in the winter stands the lonely tree,
Nor knows what birds have vanished one by
   one,
Yet knows its boughs more silent than before:
I cannot say what loves have come and gone,
I only know that summer sang in me
A little while, that in me sings no more.

Edna St. Vincent Millay

I have so often dreamed of you

I have so often dreamed of you that you
   become unreal.
Is it still time enough to reach that living body
   and to kiss on that mouth the birth of the
   voice so dear to me?
I have so often dreamed of you that my arms
   used as they are to meet on my breast in
   embracing your shadow would perhaps not
   fit the contour of your body.
And, before the real appearance of what has
   haunted and ruled me for days and years,
   I might become only a shadow.
Oh the weighing of sentiment.
I have so often dreamed of you that there
   is probably no time now to waken. I sleep
   standing, my body exposed to all the
   appearances of life and love and you, who
   alone still matter to me, I could less easily
   touch your forehead and your lips than the
   first lips and the first forehead I might meet
   by chance.
I have so often dreamed of you, walked,
   spoken, slept with your phantom that

perhaps I can be nothing any longer than a phantom among phantoms and a hundred times more shadow than the shadow which walks and will walk joyously over the sundial of your life.

Robert Desnos

Remember

Remember me when I am gone away,
   Gone far away into the silent land;
   When you can no more hold me by the
     hand,
Nor I half turn to go yet turning stay.
Remember me when no more day by day
   You tell me of our future that you plann'd:
   Only remember me; you understand
It will be late to counsel then or pray.
Yet if you should forget me for a while
   And afterwards remember, do not grieve:
   For if the darkness and corruption leave
   A vestige of the thoughts that once I had,
Better by far you should forget and smile
   Than that you should remember and be
     sad.

Christina Rossetti

The Ghost

I went back to the clanging city,
I went back where my old loves stayed,
But my heart was full of my new love's glory,
My eyes were laughing and unafraid.

I met one who had loved me madly
And told his love for all to hear –
But we talked of a thousand things together,
The past was buried too deep to fear.

I met the other, whose love was given
With never a kiss and scarcely a word –
Oh, it was then the terror took me
Of words unuttered that breathed and stirred.

Oh, love that lives its life with laughter
Or love that lives its life with tears
Can die – but love that is never spoken
Goes like a ghost through the winding
    years . . .

I went back to the clanging city,
I went back where my old loves stayed,
My heart was full of my new love's glory, –
But my eyes were suddenly afraid.

Sara Teasdale

FAREWELL TO THEE,
BUT NOT FAREWELL

#BREAKUP

When We Two Parted

When we two parted
    In silence and tears,
Half broken-hearted
    To sever for years,
Pale grew thy cheek and cold,
    Colder thy kiss;
Truly that hour foretold
    Sorrow to this.

The dew of the morning
    Sunk chill on my brow—
It felt like the warning
    Of what I feel now.
Thy vows are all broken,
    And light is thy fame;
I hear thy name spoken,
    And share in its shame.

They name thee before me,
    A knell to mine ear;
A shudder comes o'er me—
    Why wert thou so dear?

They know not I knew thee,
    Who knew thee too well—
Long, long shall I rue thee,
    Too deeply to tell.

In secret we met—
    In silence I grieve,
That thy heart could forget,
    Thy spirit deceive.
If I should meet thee
    After long years,
How should I greet thee?—
    With silence and tears.

George, Lord Byron

Little Heartbreak

A little heartbreak, wan and sore,
was sitting by herself. A sunbeam
slipped around the door and danced upon
a shelf. Though little Heartbreak knew
not why, she ceased, quite suddenly, to
cry. Still little Heartbreak sat alone.
"I never will be whole again," thus said
she in her saddest tone, "I never will be
healed of pain." Then, unannounced, a
little breeze that had been playing in the
trees, passed softly over Heartbreak's
face, and, lo! of tears there was no trace.
Then when a bird began to sing, and
Heartbreak couldn't help but hear, there
happened such a curious thing—a silvern
echo did appear, enthroned itself in
Heartbreak's breast and, like the bird,
sang with sweet zest! So little Heart-
break tossed her head and laughed to
find the world so fair. "It's true," she
cried, "my heart has bled, and I have

lived with black despair. But I can't
be quite broken, long—with sunbeams,
zephyrs, and birds' song!"

Wilhelmina Stitch

None ever was in love with me but grief

None ever was in love with me but grief.
    She wooed my from the day that I was
      born;
She stole my playthings first, the jealous thief,
    And left me there forlorn.

The birds that in my garden would have sung,
    She scared away with her unending moan;
She slew my lovers too when I was young,
    And left me there alone.

Grief, I have cursed thee often—now at last
    To hate thy name I am no longer free;
Caught in thy bony arms and prisoned fast,
    I love no love but thee.

Mary Elizabeth Coleridge

Endorsement to the Deed of Separation in the April of 1816

A year ago you swore, fond she!
    'To love, to honour', and so forth:
Such was the vow you pledged to me,
    And here's exactly what 'tis worth.

George, Lord Byron

After Soufriere

It is not grief or pain;
But like the even dropping of the rain
That thou are gone.
It is not like a grave
To weep upon;
But like the rise and falling of a wave
When the vessel's gone.

It is like the sudden void
When the city is destroyed,
Where the sun shone:
There is neither grief or pain,
But the wide waste come again.

Michael Field

In the Vaulted Way

In the vaulted way, where the passage turned
To the shadowy corner that none could see,
You paused for our parting, – plaintively:
Though overnight had come words that
    burned
My fond frail happiness out of me.

And then I kissed you, – despite my thought
That our spell must end when reflection came
On what you had deemed me, whose one long
    aim
Had been to serve you; that what I sought
Lay not in a heart that could breathe such
    blame.

But yet I kissed you: whereon you again
As of old kissed me. Why, why was it so?
Do you cleave to me after that light-tongued
    blow?
If you scorned me at eventide, how love then?
The thing is dark, Dear. I do not know.

Thomas Hardy

Since there's no help,
come let us kiss and part

Since there's no help, come let us kiss and
  part,
Nay, I have done: you get no more of me,
And I am glad, yea glad with all my heart,
That thus so cleanly, I my self can free,
Shake hands for ever, cancel all our vows,
And when we meet at any time again,
Be it not seen in either of our brows,
That we one jot of former love retain;
Now at the last gasp, of love's latest breath,
When his pulse failing, passion speechless lies,
When faith is kneeling by his bed of death,
And innocence is closing up his eyes,
    Now if thou wouldst, when all have given
      him over,
    From death to life, thou mightst him yet
      recover.

Michael Drayton

Shake hands, we shall never be friends, all's over

Shake hands, we shall never be friends, all's
    over;
    I only vex you the more I try.
All's wrong that ever I've done or said,
And nought to help it in this dull head:
    Shake hands, here's luck, good-bye.

But if you come to a road where danger
    Or guilt or anguish or shame's to share,
Be good to the lad that loves you true
And the soul that was born to die for you,
    And whistle and I'll be there.

A. E. Housman

He would not stay for me, and who can wonder?

He would not stay for me, and who can
   wonder?
     He would not stay for me to stand and
     gaze.
I shook his hand, and tore my heart in sunder,
     And went with half my life about my
     ways.

A. E. Housman

The Loss of Love

All through an empty place I go,
And find her not in any room;
The candles and the lamps I light
Go down before a wind of gloom.
Thick-spraddled lies the dust about,
A fit, sad place to write her name
Or draw her face the way she looked
That legendary night she came.

The old house crumbles bit by bit;
Each day I hear the ominous thud
That says another rent is there
For winds to pierce and storms to flood.

My orchards groan and sag with fruit;
Where, Indian-wise, the bees go round;
I let it rot upon the bough;
I eat what falls upon the ground.

The heavy cows go laboring
In agony with clotted teats;
My hands are slack; my blood is cold;
I marvel that my heart still beats.

I have no will to weep or sing,
No least desire to pray or curse;
The loss of love is a terrible thing;
They lie who say that death is worse.

Countee Cullen

Goodbye

So we must say Goodbye, my darling,
And go, as lovers go, for ever;
Tonight remains, to pack and fix on labels
And make an end of lying down together.

I put a final shilling in the gas,
And watch you slip your dress below your
  knees
And lie so still I hear your rustling comb
Modulate the autumn in the trees.

And all the countless things I shall remember
Lay mummy-cloths of silence round my head;
I fill the carafe with a drink of water;
You say 'We paid a guinea for this bed,'

And then, 'We'll leave some gas, a little
  warmth
For the next resident, and these dry flowers,'
And turn your face away, afraid to speak
The big word, that Eternity is ours.

Your kisses close my eyes and yet you stare
As though god struck a child with nameless
    fears;
Perhaps the water glitters and discloses
Time's chalice and its limpid useless tears.

Everything we renounce except our selves;
Selfishness is the last of all to go;
Our sighs are exhalations of the earth,
Our footprints leave a track across the snow.

We made the universe to be our home,
Our nostrils took the wind to be our breath,
Our hearts are massive towers of delight,
We stride across the seven seas of death.

Yet when all's done you'll keep the emerald
I placed upon your finger in the street;
And I will keep the patches that you sewed
On my old battledress tonight, my sweet.

Alun Lewis

The Last Ride Together

I

I said – Then, dearest, since 'tis so,
Since now at length my fate I know,
Since nothing all my love avails,
Since all, my life seemed meant for, fails,
    Since this was written and needs must
      be –
My whole heart rises up to bless
Your name in pride and thankfulness!
Take back the hope you gave, – I claim
Only a memory of the same,
– And this beside, if you will not blame,
    Your leave for one more last ride with me.

II

My mistress bent that brow of hers;
Those deep dark eyes where pride demurs
When pity would be softening through,
Fixed me a breathing-while or two
    With life or death in the balance: right!
The blood replenished me again;

My last thought was at least not vain:
I and my mistress, side by side
Shall be together, breathe and ride,
So, one day more am I deified.
    Who knows but the world may end
        tonight?

III

Hush! if you saw some western cloud
All billowy-bosomed, over-bowed
By many benedictions – sun's
And moon's and evening-star's at once–
    And so, you, looking and loving best,
Conscious grew, your passion drew
Cloud, sunset, moonrise, star-shine too,
Down on you, near and yet more near,
Till flesh must fade for heaven was here!–
Thus leant she and lingered – joy and fear!
    Thus lay she a moment on my breast.

IV

Then we began to ride. My soul
Smoothed itself out, a long-cramped scroll
Freshening and fluttering in the wind.

Fast hopes already lay behind.
      What need to strive with a life awry?
Had I said that, had I done this,
So might I gain, so might I miss.
Might she have loved me? just as well
She might have hated, who can tell!
Where had I been now if the worst befell?
      And here we are riding, she and I.

V

Fail I alone, in words and deeds?
Why, all men strive and who succeeds?
We rode; it seemed my spirit flew,
Saw other regions, cities new,
      As the world rushed by on either side.
I thought, – All labour, yet no less
Bear up beneath their unsuccess.
Look at the end of work, contrast
The petty done, the undone vast,
This present of theirs with the hopeful past!
      I hoped she would love me; here we ride.

VI

What hand and brain went ever paired?
What heart alike conceived and dared?
What act proved all its thought had been?
What will but felt the fleshly screen?
    We ride and I see her bosom heave.
There's many a crown for who can reach.
Ten lines, a statesman's life in each!
The flag stuck on a heap of bones,
A soldier's doing! what atones?
They scratch his name on the Abbey-stones.
    My riding is better, by their leave.

VII

What does it all mean, poet? Well,
Your brains beat into rhythm, you tell
What we felt only; you expressed
You hold things beautiful the best,
    And pace them in rhyme so, side by side.
'Tis something, nay 'tis much: but then,
Have you yourself what's best for men?
Are you – poor, sick, old ere your time –

Nearer one whit your own sublime
Than we who never have turned a rhyme?
　　Sing, riding's a joy! For me, I ride.

VIII

And you, great sculptor – so, you gave
A score of years to Art, her slave,
And that's your Venus, whence we turn
To yonder girl that fords the burn!
　　You acquiesce, and shall I repine?
What, man of music, you grown grey
With notes and nothing else to say,
Is this your sole praise from a friend,
'Greatly his opera's strains intend,
But in music we know how fashions end!'
　　I gave my youth; but we ride, in fine.

IX

Who knows what's fit for us? Had fate
Proposed bliss here should sublimate
My being – had I signed the bond –
Still one must lead some life beyond,
　　Have a bliss to die with, dim-descried.

This foot once planted on the goal,
This glory-garland round my soul,
Could I descry such? Try and test!
I sink back shuddering from the quest.
Earth being so good, would heaven seem best?
    Now, heaven and she are beyond this ride.

X

And yet – she has not spoke so long!
What if heaven be that, fair and strong
At life's best, with our eyes upturned
Whither life's flower is first discerned,
    We, fixed so, ever should so abide?
What if we still ride on, we two
With life for ever old yet new,
Changed not in kind but in degree,
The instant made eternity,–
And heaven just prove that I and she
    Ride, ride together, for ever ride?

Robert Browning

Good-Bye!

Good-bye, good-bye!
And one goes out, and one stays standing still,
And that day's sun sink, o'er the low green
  hill.

Good-bye, good-bye!
And he goes on, far over field and moor,
And she turns back, goes in, and shuts the
  door.

Good-bye, good-bye!
She smiled upon him to the very last;
He'll never know what came when that was
  past.

Good-bye, good-bye!
And he who goes—he has but half the pain,
His world is new, her empty rooms remain.

Good-bye, good-bye!
The books he opened, can she bear to close?
The rose he gathered; she will keep that rose!

Good-bye, good-bye!
And yet a day shall come when she shall say
"'T was well that he who loved me went
   away."

Good-bye, good-bye!
Love scarce is true until it has been tried;
And hearts can hold when hands are severed
   wide.

Good-bye, good-bye!
The last strong light of love in dying eyes
Pierces the mists of death that o'er them rise.

Good-bye, good-bye!
Nor Life nor Death has power to sever Love
It moves the world and builds the heaven
   above.

Good-bye, good-bye!
It ever has a sound of tears and sorrow;
Yet while we sleep, it changes to
   "Good-morrow."

Isabella Fyvie Mayo

Farewell

Farewell to thee! but not farewell
To all my fondest thoughts of thee:
Within my heart they still shall dwell;
And they shall cheer and comfort me.
O, beautiful, and full of grace!
If thou hadst never met mine eye,
I had not dreamed a living face
Could fancied charms so far outvie.

If I may ne'er behold again
That form and face so dear to me,
Nor hear thy voice, still would I fain
Preserve, for aye, their memory.

That voice, the magic of whose tone
Can wake an echo in my breast,
Creating feelings that, alone,
Can make my tranced spirit blest.

That laughing eye, whose sunny beam
My memory would not cherish less; –
And oh, that smile! whose joyous gleam
Nor mortal language can express.

Adieu, but let me cherish, still,
The hope with which I cannot part.
Contempt may wound, and coldness chill,
But still it lingers in my heart.

And who can tell but Heaven, at last,
May answer all my thousand prayers,
And bid the future pay the past
With joy for anguish, smiles for tears?

Anne Brontë

AND WE'LL LIVE OUR
WHOLE YOUNG LIVES AWAY
IN THE JOYS OF A LIVING LOVE

#YOUANDI4EVA

Married Love

You and I
Have so much love
That it
Burns like a fire,
In which we bake a lump of clay
Molded into a figure of you
And a figure of me.
Then we take both of them,
And break them into pieces,
And mix the pieces with water,
And mold again a figure of you,
And a figure of me.
I am in your clay.
You are in my clay.
In life we share a single quilt.
In death we will share one bed.

Guan Tao-Sheng

I Love You

I love your lips when they're wet with wine
And red with a wild desire;
I love your eyes when the lovelight lies
Lit with a passionate fire.
I love your arms when the warm white flesh
Touches mine in a fond embrace;
I love your hair when the strands enmesh
Your kisses against my face.

Not for me the cold, calm kiss
Of a virgin's bloodless love;
Not for me the saint's white bliss,
Nor the heart of a spotless dove.
But give me the love that so freely gives
And laughs at the whole world's blame,
With your body so young and warm in my
    arms,
It sets my poor heart aflame.

So kiss me sweet with your warm wet mouth,
Still fragrant with ruby wine,
And say with a fervor born of the South
That your body and soul are mine.

Clasp me close in your warm young arms,
While the pale stars shine above,
And we'll live our whole young lives away
In the joys of a living love.

Ella Wheeler Wilcox

A Lover's Quarrel

We two were lovers, the Sea and I;
We plighted our troth 'neath a summer sky.

And all through the riotous, ardent weather
We dreamed, and loved, and rejoiced together.

.   .   .   .   .   .

At times my lover would rage and storm.
I said: 'No matter, his heart is warm.'

Whatever his humour, I loved his ways,
And so we lived through the golden days.

I know not the manner it came about,
But in the autumn we two fell out.

Yet this I know–'twas the fault of the Sea,
And was not my fault, that he changed to me.

.   .   .   .   .   .

I lingered as long as a woman may
To find what her lover will do or say.

But he met my smiles with a sullen frown,
And so I turned to the wooing Town.

Oh, bold was this suitor, and blithe as bold!
His look was as bright as the Sea's was cold.

As the Sea was sullen, the Town was gay;
He made me forget for a winter day.

For a winter day and a winter night
He laughed my sorrow away from sight.

And yet, in spite of his mirth and cheer,
I knew full well he was insincere.

And when the young buds burst on the tree,
The old love woke in my heart for the Sea.

Pride was forgotten–I knew, I knew,
That the soul of the Sea, like my own, was
    true.

I heard him calling, and lo! I came,
To find him waiting, for ever the same.

And when he saw me, with murmurs sweet
He ran to meet me, and fell at my feet.

And so again 'neath a summer sky
We have plighted our troth, the Sea and I.

Ella Wheeler Wilcox

I loved you first: but afterwards your love

'Poca favilla gran fiamma seconda.' *Dante*

'Ogni altra cosa, ogni pensier va fore,
E sol ivi con voi rimansi amore.' *Petrarca*

I loved you first: but afterwards your love
    Outsoaring mine, sang such a loftier song
As drowned the friendly cooings of my dove.
    Which owes the other most? my love was
       long,
    And yours one moment seemed to wax
       more strong;
I loved and guessed at you, you construed me
And loved me for what might or might not
be—
    Nay, weights and measures do us both a
       wrong.
For verily love knows not 'mine' or 'thine;'
    With separate 'I' and 'thou' free love has
       done,
        For one is both and both are one in
        love:

Rich love knows nought of 'thine that is not
   mine;'
            Both have the strength and both the
            length thereof,
Both of us, of the love which makes us
   one.

Christina Rossetti

Love not me for comely grace

Love not me for comely grace,
For my pleasing eye or face;
Nor for any outward part,
No, nor for my constant heart:
 For those may fail or turn to ill,
  So thou and I shall sever.
Keep therefore a true woman's eye,
And love me still, but know not why;
 So hast thou the same reason still
 To doat upon me ever.

John Wilbye

My Wife

Trusty, dusky, vivid, true,
With eyes of gold and bramble-dew,
Steel true and blade-straight,
The great artificer
Made my mate.

Honour, anger, valour, fire,
A love that life could never tire,
Death quench or evil stir;
The mighty master
Gave to her.

Teacher, tender, comrade, wife,
A fellow-farer true through life,
Heart-whole and soul-free,
The august father
Gave to me.

Robert Louis Stevenson

My True Love Hath My Heart

My true-love hath my heart and I have his,
By just exchange one for the other given:
I hold his dear, and mine he cannot miss;
There never was a bargain better driven.
His heart in me keeps me and him in one;
My heart in him his thoughts and senses
    guides:
He loves my heart, for once it was his own;
I cherish his because in me it bides.
His heart his wound received from my sight;
My heart was wounded with his wounded
    heart;
For as from me on him his hurt did light,
So still, methought, in me his hurt did smart:
Both equal hurt, in this change sought our
    bliss,
My true love hath my heart and I have his.

Sir Philip Sidney

Sonnet 44

Beloved, thou hast brought me many flowers
Plucked in the garden, all the summer through
And winter, and it seemed as if they grew
In this close room, nor missed the sun and
    showers,
So, in the like name of that love of ours,
Take back these thoughts which here unfolded
    too,
And which on warm and cold days I withdrew
From my heart's ground. Indeed, those beds
    and bowers
Be overgrown with bitter weeds and rue,
And wait thy weeding; yet here's eglantine,
Here's ivy!—take them, as I used to do
Thy flowers, and keep them where they shall
    not pine.
Instruct thine eyes to keep their colours true,
And tell thy soul, their roots are left in mine.

Elizabeth Barrett Browning

This Day

This day, this day alone, is yours and mine.
Yesterday, with its mistakes and faults, is past.
And of tomorrow there is no certain sign.
Today is ours. Welcome and hold it fast.
We have, each one, a special part to play,
seeming so small to our impatient eyes,
but we must face the duty of To-day—
think you the sun resents that he must rise;
or the moon weary of her ministry;
or the stars falter on their destined way;
or the sap fail to vitalize the tree;
shall we refuse the task that's ours, To-day?
The moon is beautiful in her bright shining;
the sun majestic in his robe of red.
Hush! they must never hear a human whining!
Too soon, too soon, will this good day have
    fled.
Stars, sun and moon and the majestic sea,
teach us the spirit of your service, pray!
Then we will face with quiet serenity,
with eager will, with joyous pride—To-day.

Wilhelmina Stitch

Unending Love

I seem to have loved you in numberless forms,
   numberless times . . .
In life after life, in age after age, forever.
My spellbound heart has made and remade
   the necklace of songs,
That you take as a gift, wear round your neck
   in your many forms,
In life after life, in age after age, forever.

Whenever I hear old chronicles of love, its
   age-old pain,
Its ancient tale of being apart or together.
As I stare on and on into the past, in the end
   you emerge,
Clad in the light of a pole-star piercing the
   darkness of time:
You become an image of what is remembered
   forever.

You and I have floated here on the stream that
   brings from the fount.
At the heart of time, love of one for another.

We have played alongside millions of lovers,
    shared in the same
Shy sweetness of meeting, the same distressful
    tears of farewell-
Old love but in shapes that renew and renew
    forever.

Today it is heaped at your feet, it has found its
    end in you
The love of all man's days both past and
    forever:
Universal joy, universal sorrow, universal life.
The memories of all loves merging with this
    one love of ours –
And the songs of every poet past and forever.

Rabindranath Tagore

I SO LIKED YOU

#THEONETHATGOTAWAY
#STILLITHINKOFYOU

Time does not bring relief;
you all have lied

Time does not bring relief; you all have lied
Who told me time would ease me of my pain!
I miss him in the weeping of the rain;
I want him at the shrinking of the tide;
The old snows melt from every mountain-side,
And last year's leaves are smoke in every lane;
But last year's bitter loving must remain
Heaped on my heart, and my old thoughts
    abide.
There are a hundred places where I fear
To go,—so with his memory they brim.
And entering with relief some quiet place
Where never fell his foot or shone his face
I say, "There is no memory of him here!"
And so stand stricken, so remembering him.

Edna St. Vincent Millay

Sometimes with One I Love

Sometimes with one I love I fill myself with
    rage for fear I effuse unreturn'd love,
But now I think there is no unreturn'd love,
    the pay is certain one way or another,
(I loved a certain person ardently and my love
    was not return'd,
Yet out of that I have written these songs.)

Walt Whitman

How Can I Forget

That farewell voice of love is never heard
   again,
Yet I remember it and think on it with pain:
I see the place she spoke when passing by,
The flowers were blooming as her form drew
   nigh,
That voice is gone, with every pleasing tone –
Loved but one moment and the next alone.
'Farewell' the winds repeated as she went
Walking in silence through the grassy bent;
The wild flowers – they ne'er looked so sweet
   before –
Bowed in farewells to her they'll see no more.
In this same spot the wild flowers bloom the
   same
In scent and hue and shape, ay, even name.
'Twas here she said farewell and no one yet
Has so sweet spoken – How can I forget?

John Clare

I Do Not Love Thee

I do not love thee!–no! I do not love thee!
And yet when thou art absent I am sad;
    And envy even the bright blue sky above
      thee,
Whose quiet stars may see thee and be glad.

I do not love thee!–yet, I know not why,
Whate'er thou dost seems still well done,
  to me:
    And often in my solitude I sigh
That those I do love are not more like thee!

I do not love thee!–yet, when thou art gone,
I hate the sound (though those who speak be
  dear)
    Which breaks the lingering echo of the
      tone
Thy voice of music leaves upon my ear.

I do not love thee!–yet thy speaking eyes,
With their deep, bright, and most expressive
  blue,

Between me and the midnight heaven
    arise,
Oftener than any eyes I ever knew.

I know I do not love thee! yet, alas!
Others will scarcely trust my candid heart;
    And oft I catch them smiling as they pass,
Because they see me gazing where thou art.

Caroline Elizabeth Sarah Norton

Vain Hope

Sometimes, to solace my sad heart, I say,
Though late it be, though lily-time be past,
Though all the summer skies be overcast,
Haply I will go down to her, some day,
And cast my rests of life before her feet,
That she may have her will of me, being so
    sweet
And none gainsay!

So might she look on me with pitying eyes,
And lay calm hands of healing on my head;
"Because of thy long pains be comforted;
For I, even I, am Love; sad soul, arise!"
So, for her graciousness, I might at last
Gaze on the very face of Love, and hold him
    fast
In no disguise.

Haply, I said, she will take pity on me,
Though late I come, long after lily-time,
With burden of waste days and drifted rhyme:

Her kind, calm eyes, down drooping maidenly,
Shall change, grow soft: there is yet time,
   meseems,
I said, for solace; though I know these things
   are dreams,
And may not be!

Ernest Dowson

Worn Out

Thy strong arms are around me, love
    My head is on thy breast;
Low words of comfort come from thee
    Yet my soul has no rest.

For I am but a startled thing
    Nor can I ever be
Aught save a bird whose broken wing
    Must fly away from thee.

I cannot give to thee the love
    I gave so long ago,
The love that turned and struck me down
    Amid the blinding snow.

I can but give a failing heart
    And weary eyes of pain,
A faded mouth that cannot smile
    And may not laugh again.

Yet keep thine arms around me, love,
    Until I fall to sleep;
Then leave me, saying no goodbye
    Lest I might wake, and weep.

Lizzie Siddal

I Loved You

I loved you; even now I may confess,
  Some embers of my love their fire retain;
But do not let it cause you more distress,
  I do not want to sadden you again.
Hopeless and tonguetied, yet I loved you
  dearly
  With pangs the jealous and timid know;
So tenderly I loved you, so sincerely,
  I pray God grant another love you so.

Alexander Pushkin

One Night

The room was cheap and sordid,
hidden above the suspect taverna.
From the window you could see the alley,
dirty and narrow. From below
came the voices of workmen
playing cards, enjoying themselves.

And there on that ordinary, plain bed
I had love's body, knew those intoxicating lips,
red and sensual,
red lips so intoxicating
that now as I write, after so many years,
in my lonely house, I'm drunk with passion
   again.

Constantine P. Cavafy

When They Come Alive

Try to preserve them, poet,
your visions of love,
however few may stay for you.
Cast them, half hidden, into your verse.
Try to hold on to them, poet,
when they come alive in your mind
at night or in the brightness of noon.

Constantine P. Cavafy

Sonnet 16

Long have I long'd to see my love againe,
    Still have I wisht, but never could
      obtaine it;
    Rather than all the world (if I might
      gaine it)
Would I desire my love's sweet precious gaine.
Yet in my soule I see him everie day,
    See him, and see his still sterne
      countenaunce,
    But (ah) what is of long continuance,
Where majestie and beautie beares the sway?
Sometimes, when I imagine that I see him,
    (As love is full of foolish fantasies)
    Weening to kisse his lips, as my love's
      fees,
I feele but aire: nothing but aire to bee him.
    Thus with Ixion, kisse I clouds in vaine:
    Thus with Ixion, feele I endles paine.

Richard Barnfield

At Tea

The kettle descants in a cozy drone,
And the young wife looks in her husband's
    face,
And then at her guest's, and shows in her own
Her sense that she fills an envied place;
And the visiting lady is all abloom,
And says there was never so sweet a room.

And the happy young housewife does not
    know
That the woman beside her was first his
    choice,
Till the fates ordained it could not be so . . .
Betraying nothing in look or voice
The guest sits smiling and sips her tea,
And he throws her a stray glance yearningly.

Thomas Hardy

I think I should have loved you presently

I think I should have loved you presently,
And given in earnest words I flung in jest;
And lifted honest eyes for you to see,
And caught your hand against my cheek and
   breast;
And all my pretty follies flung aside
That won you to me, and beneath your gaze,
Naked of reticence and shorn of pride,
Spread like a chart my little wicked ways.
I, that had been to you, had you remained,
But one more waking from a recurrent dream,
Cherish no less the certain stakes I gained,
And walk your memory's halls, austere,
   supreme,
A ghost in marble of a girl you knew
Who would have loved you in a day or two

Edna St. Vincent Millay

White Heliotrope

The feverish room and that white bed,
The tumbled skirts upon a chair,
The novel flung half-open, where
Hat, hair-pins, puffs, and paints are spread;

The mirror that has sucked your face
Into its secret deep of deeps,
And there mysteriously keeps
Forgotten memories of grace;

And you half dressed and half awake,
Your slant eyes strangely watching me,
And I, who watch you drowsily,
With eyes that, having slept not, ache;

This (need one dread? nay, dare one hope?)
Will rise, a ghost of memory, if
Ever again my handkerchief
Is scented with White Heliotrope.

Arthur Symons

The Shortest and Sweetest of Songs

Come
Home.

George MacDonald

I so liked Spring last year

I so liked Spring last year
Because you were here; –
The thrushes too –
Because it was these you so liked to hear –
I so liked you.

This year's a different thing, –
I'll not think of you.
But I'll like the Spring because it is simply
    Spring
As the thrushes do.

Charlotte Mew

If you were coming in the Fall

If you were coming in the Fall,
I'd brush the Summer by
With half a smile, and half a spurn,
As Housewives do, a Fly.

If I could see you in a year,
I'd wind the months in balls –
And put them each in separate Drawers,
For fear the numbers fuse –

If only Centuries, delayed,
I'd count them on my Hand,
Subtracting, till my fingers dropped
Into Van Dieman's Land.

If certain, when this life was out –
That yours and mine, should be
I'd toss it yonder, like a Rind,
And take Eternity –

But, now, uncertain of the length
Of this, that is between,
It goads me, like the Goblin Bee –
That will not state – its sting.

Of Course – I prayed –
And did God Care?
He cared as much as on the Air
A Bird – had stamped her foot –
And cried "Give Me" –
My Reason – Life –
I had not had – but for Yourself –
'Twere better Charity
To leave me in the Atom's Tomb –
Merry, and Nought, and gay, and numb –
Than this smart Misery.

Emily Dickinson

I LONGED FOR YOU WITH YOUR
MANTLE OF LOVE TO FOLD ME
OVER, AND DRIVE FROM OUT OF
MY BODY THE DEEP COLD THAT
HAD SUNK TO MY SOUL,
AND THERE KEPT HOLD

#CUFFINGSEASON

Autumn Song

I

Soon we'll plunge into the bitter shadows:
Goodbye bright sunlit summers, all too short!
Already I can hear the gloomy blows:
the wood reverberates in some paved court.

Winter once more will enter in my being:
   anger,
shuddering, horror, hate, forced labour's
   shock,
like the sun in its deep hell, northern, polar,
my heart no more than a red, frozen block.

Trembling, I hear every log that falls:
building a scaffold makes no duller echoes.
My spirit's like a shattered tower, its walls
split by the battering ram's slow tireless blows.

Rocked by monotonous thuds, I feel it's done,
a coffin's being nailed in haste somewhere.

For whom? – Yesterday summer, now it's
   autumn!
The mysterious noise rings of departure there.

II

I love the greenish light of your almond eyes,
gentle beauty, but all's bitter to me today,
and nothing, your love, the boudoir, your fire,
matches the sun, for me, glittering on the
   waves.

Yet tender heart, love me still! Be like a
   mother
however ungrateful, however unworthy I am:
be the short-lived sweetness, sister or lover,
of a glorious autumn or the setting sun.

Short task! The grave waits: it is greedy!
Ah, let me rest my forehead on your knees,
regretting summer, white and torrid, let me
enjoy the late season's gentle yellow rays!

Charles Baudelaire

Coldness in Love

And you remember, in the afternoon
The sea and the sky went grey, as if there had
  sunk
A flocculent dust on the floor of the world: the
  festoon
Of the sky sagged dusty as spider cloth,
And coldness clogged the sea, till it ceased to
  croon.

A dank, sickening scent came up from the
  grime
Of weed that blackened the shore, so that I
  recoiled
Feeling the raw cold dun me: and all the time
You leapt about on the slippery rocks, and
  threw
Me words that rang with a brassy, shallow
  chime.

And all day long, that raw and ancient cold
Deadened me through, till the grey downs
  dulled to sleep.

Then I longed for you with your mantle of
    love to fold
Me over, and drive from out of my body the
    deep
Cold that had sunk to my soul, and there kept
    hold.

But still to me all evening long you were cold,
And I was numb with a bitter, deathly ache;
Till old days drew me back into their fold,
And dim hopes crowded me warm with
    companionship,
And memories clustered me close, and sleep
    was cajoled.

And I slept till dawn at the window blew in
    like dust,
Like a linty, raw-cold dust disturbed from the
    floor
Of the unswept sea; a grey pale light like must
That settled upon my face and hands till it
    seemed
To flourish there, as pale mould blooms on a
    crust.

And I rose in fear, needing you fearfully.
For I thought you were warm as a sudden jet
  of blood.
I thought I could plunge in your living
  hotness, and be
Clean of the cold and the must. With my hand
  on the latch
I heard you in your sleep speak strangely
  to me.

And I dared not enter, feeling suddenly
  dismayed.
So I went and washed my deadened flesh in
  the sea
And came back tingling clean, but worn and
  frayed
With cold, like the shell of the moon; and
  strange it seems
That my love can dawn in warmth again,
  unafraid.

D. H. Lawrence

Silent is the House

Come, the wind may never again
Blow as it now blows for us;
And the stars may never again shine as now
   they shine;
Long before October returns,
Seas of blood will have parted us;
And you must crush the love in your heart, and
   I the love in mine!

Emily Brontë

On Rainy Weather

Perhaps you love, much less than me, these
  storms.
Could be. The mind will vary in its forms.

Marcel Proust

XLVI

Even in the moment of our earliest kiss,
When sighed the straitened bud into the
   flower,
Sat the dry seed of most unwelcome this;
And that I knew, though not the day and hour.
Too season-wise am I, being country-bred,
To tilt at autumn or defy the frost:
Snuffing the chill even as my fathers did,
I say with them, "What's out tonight is lost."
I only hoped, with the mild hope of all
Who watch the leaf take shape upon the tree,
A fairer summer and a later fall
Than in these parts a man is apt to see,
And sunny clusters ripened for the wine:
I tell you this across the blackened vine.

Edna St. Vincent Millay

Winter: My Secret

I tell my secret? No indeed, not I:
Perhaps some day, who knows?
But not today; it froze, and blows, and snows,
And you're too curious: fie!
You want to hear it? well:
Only, my secret's mine, and I won't tell.

Or, after all, perhaps there's none:
Suppose there is no secret after all,
But only just my fun.
Today's a nipping day, a biting day;
In which one wants a shawl,
A veil, a cloak, and other wraps:
I cannot ope to every one who taps,
And let the draughts come whistling thro' my
    hall;
Come bounding and surrounding me,
Come buffeting, astounding me,
Nipping and clipping thro' my wraps and all.
I wear my mask for warmth: who ever shows
His nose to Russian snows
To be pecked at by every wind that blows?

You would not peck? I thank you for good
   will,
Believe, but leave that truth untested still.

Spring's an expansive time: yet I don't trust
March with its peck of dust,
Nor April with its rainbow-crowned brief
   showers,
Nor even May, whose flowers
One frost may wither thro' the sunless hours.

Perhaps some languid summer day,
When drowsy birds sing less and less,
And golden fruit is ripening to excess,
If there's not too much sun nor too much cloud,
And the warm wind is neither still nor loud,
Perhaps my secret I may say,
Or you may guess.

Christina Rossetti

Never the Time and the Place

Never the time and the place
And the loved one all together!
This path—how soft to pace!
This May—what magic weather!
Where is the loved one's face?
In a dream that loved one's face meets
   mine,
But the house is narrow, the place is bleak
Where, outside, rain and wind combine
With a furtive ear, if I strive to speak,
With a hostile eye at my flushing cheek,
With a malice that marks each word,
   each sign!
O enemy sly and serpentine,
Uncoil thee from the waking man!
Do I hold the Past
Thus firm and fast
Yet doubt if the Future hold I can?
This path so soft to pace shall lead
Thro' the magic of May to herself indeed!
Or narrow if needs the house must be,

Outside are the storms and strangers: we
Oh, close, safe, warm sleep I and she,—
I and she!

Robert Browning

The Falling of the Leaves

Autumn is over the long leaves that love us,
And over the mice in the barley sheaves;
Yellow the leaves of the rowan above us,
And yellow the wet wild-strawberry leaves.

The hour of the waning of love has beset us,
And weary and worn are our sad souls now;
Let us part, ere the season of passion forget us,
With a kiss and a tear on thy drooping brow.

W. B. Yeats

Thaw

Over the land freckled with snow half-thawed
The speculating rooks at their nests cawed
And saw from elm-tops, delicate as flowers of
   grass,
What we below could not see, Winter pass.

Edward Thomas

ARE YOU LOVING ENOUGH?

#ADVICE

When I was one-and-twenty

When I was one-and-twenty
I heard a wise man say,
'Give crowns and pounds and guineas
But not your heart away;
Give pearls away and rubies
But keep your fancy free,'
But I was one-and-twenty,
No use to talk to me.

When I was one-and-twenty
I heard him say again,
'The heart out of the bosom
Was never given in vain;
'Tis paid with sighs a plenty
And sold for endless rue.'
And I am two-and-twenty
And oh, 'tis true, 'tis true.

A. E. Housman

Do Not Love Too Long

Sweetheart, do not love too long:
I loved long and long,
And grew to be out of fashion
Like an old song.

All through the years of our youth
Neither could have known
Their own thought from the other's,
We were so much at one.

But O, in a minute she changed –
O do not love too long,
Or you will grow out of fashion
Like an old song.

W. B. Yeats

Solitude

Laugh, and the world laughs with you;
 Weep, and you weep alone,
For sad old earth must borrow its mirth,
 But has trouble enough of its own.
Sing, and the hills will answer;
 Sigh, it is lost on the air,
The echoes bound to a joyful sound,
 But shrink from voicing care.

Rejoice, and men will seek you;
 Grieve, and they turn and go.
They want full measure of all your pleasure,
 But they do not need your woe.
Be glad, and your friends are many;
 Be sad, and you lose them all—
There are none to decline your nectar'd wine,
 But alone you must drink life's gall.

Feast, and your halls are crowded;
 Fast, and the world goes by.
Succeed and give, and it helps you live,
 But no man can help you die.

There is room in the halls of pleasure
    For a large and lordly train,
But one by one we must all file on
    Through the narrow aisles of pain.

Ella Wheeler Wilcox

Never Give All the Heart

Never give all the heart, for love
Will hardly seem worth thinking of
To passionate women if it seem
Certain, and they never dream
That it fades out from kiss to kiss;
For everything that's lovely is
But a brief, dreamy, kind delight.
O never give the heart outright,
For they, for all smooth lips can say,
Have given their hearts up to the play.
And who could play it well enough
If deaf and dumb and blind with love?
He that made this knows all the cost,
For he gave all his heart and lost.

W. B. Yeats

How to Know Love from Deceit

Love to faults is always blind
Always is to joy inclind
Lawless wingd & unconfind
And breaks all chains from every mind

Deceit to secrecy confind
Lawful cautious & refind
To every thing but interest blind
And forges fetters for the mind

William Blake

Love and Jealousy

How much are they deceived who vainly strive,
By jealous fears, to keep our flames alive?
Love's like a torch, which if secured from
    blasts,
Will faintlier burn; but then it longer lasts.
Exposed to storms of jealousy and doubt,
The blaze grows greater, but 'tis sooner out.

William Walsh

Are You Loving Enough?

Are you loving enough? There is some one
   dear,
Some one you hold as the dearest of all
In the holiest shrine of your heart.
Are you making it known? Is the truth of it
   clear
To the one you love? If death's quick call
Should suddenly tear you apart,
Leaving no time for a long farewell,
Would you feel you had nothing to tell—
Nothing you wished you had said before
The closing of that dark door?
Are you loving enough? The swift years fly—
Oh, faster and faster they hurry away,
And each one carries its dead.
The good deed left for the by and by,
The word to be uttered another day,
May never be done or said.
Let the love word sound in the listening ear,
Nor wait to speak it above a bier.

Oh the time for telling your love is brief,
But long, long, long is the time for grief.
Are you loving enough?

Ella Wheeler Wilcox

XCVII: A Superscription

Look in my face; my name is
  Might-have-been;
    I am also called No-more, Too-late,
      Farewell;
    Unto thine ear I hold the dead-sea shell
Cast up thy Life's foam-fretted feet between;
Unto thine eyes the glass where that is seen
    Which had Life's form and Love's, but by
      my spell
    Is now a shaken shadow intolerable,
Of ultimate things unuttered the frail screen.

Mark me, how still I am! But should there
  dart
    One moment through thy soul the soft
      surprise
    Of that winged Peace which lulls the
      breath of sigh, –
Then shalt thou see me smile, and turn apart
Thy visage to mine ambush at thy heart
    Sleepless with cold commemorative eyes.

Dante Gabriel Rossetti

Love one another,
but make not a bond of love

Love one another, but make not a bond of
  love.
Let it rather be a moving sea between the
  shores of your souls.
Fill each other's cup, but drink not from one
  cup.
Give one another of your bread, but eat not
  from the same loaf.
Sing and dance together and be joyous, but let
  each one of you be alone.
Even as the strings of a lute are alone though
  they quiver with the same music.
Give your hearts, but not into each other's
  keeping.
For only the hand of life can contain your
  hearts.
And stand together, yet not too near together.
For the pillars of the temple stand apart.
And the oak tree and the cypress grow not in
  each other's shadow.

Kahlil Gibran

On the Nature of Love

The night is black and the forest has no end;
a million people thread it in a million ways.
We have trysts to keep in the darkness, but
   where
or with whom – of that we are unaware.
But we have this faith – that a lifetime's bliss
will appear any minute, with a smile upon its
   lips.
Scents, touches, sounds, snatches of songs
brush us, pass us, give us delightful shocks.
Then peradventure there's a flash of lightning:
whomever I see that instant I fall in love with.
I call that person and cry: 'This life is blest!
For your sake such miles have I traversed!'
All those others who came close and
   moved off
in the darkness – I don't know if they exist
   or not.

Rabindranath Tagore

Advice

I must do as you do? Your way I own
    Is a very good way. And still,
There are sometimes two straight roads to a
  town,
    One over, one under the hill.

You are treading the safe and the well-worn
  way,
    That the prudent choose each time;
And you think me reckless and rash to-day
    Because I prefer to climb.

Your path is the right one, and so is mine.
    We are not like peas in a pod,
Compelled to lie in a certain line,
    Or else be scattered abroad.

'Twere a dull old world, methinks, my friend,
    If we all went just one way;
Yet our paths will meet no doubt at the end,
    Though they lead apart to-day.

You like the shade, and I like the sun;
　　You like an even pace,
I like to mix with the crowd and run,
　　And then rest after the race.

I like danger, and storm and strife,
　　You like a peaceful time;
I like the passion and surge of life,
　　You like its gentle rhyme.

You like buttercups, dewy sweet,
　　And crocuses, framed in snow;
I like roses, born of the heat,
　　And the red carnation's glow.

I must live my life, not yours, my friend,
　　For so it was written down;
We must follow our given paths to the end,
　　But I trust we shall meet—in town.

Ella Wheeler Wilcox

Desiderata

Go placidly amid the noise and haste,
and remember what peace there may be in
   silence.
As far as possible without surrender
be on good terms with all persons.
Speak your truth quietly and clearly;
and listen to others,
even the dull and the ignorant;
they too have their story.

Avoid loud and aggressive persons,
they are vexations to the spirit.
If you compare yourself with others,
you may become vain and bitter;
for always there will be greater and lesser
   persons than yourself.
Enjoy your achievements as well as your plans.

Keep interested in your own career, however
   humble;
it is a real possession in the changing fortunes
   of time.
Exercise caution in your business affairs;

for the world is full of trickery.
But let this not blind you to what virtue
    there is;
many persons strive for high ideals;
and everywhere life is full of heroism.

Be yourself.
Especially, do not feign affection.
Neither be cynical about love;
for in the face of all aridity and
    disenchantment
it is as perennial as the grass.

Take kindly the counsel of the years,
gracefully surrendering the things of youth.
Nurture strength of spirit to shield you in
    sudden misfortune.
But do not distress yourself with dark
    imaginings.
Many fears are born of fatigue and loneliness.
Beyond a wholesome discipline,
be gentle with yourself.

You are a child of the universe,
no less than the trees and the stars;

you have a right to be here.
And whether or not it is clear to you,
no doubt the universe is unfolding as it should.

Therefore be at peace with God,
whatever you conceive Him to be,
and whatever your labors and aspirations,
in the noisy confusion of life keep peace with
   your soul.

With all its sham, drudgery, and broken
   dreams,
it is still a beautiful world.
Be cheerful.
Strive to be happy.

Max Ehrmann

Permissions Acknowledgements

'Their Sex Life' is published with the permission of John Ammons c/o Writers Representatives LLC, New York, NY 10011, also collected in *The Really Short Poems of A.R. Ammons*, W.W. Norton, 1991.

MACMILLAN COLLECTOR'S LIBRARY

Own the world's great works of literature in one beautiful collectible library

Designed and curated to appeal to book lovers everywhere, Macmillan Collector's Library editions are small enough to travel with you and striking enough to take pride of place on your bookshelf. These much-loved literary classics also make the perfect gift.

Beautifully produced with gilt edges, a ribbon marker, bespoke illustrated cover and real cloth binding, every Macmillan Collector's Library hardback adheres to the same high production values.

Discover something new or cherish your favourite stories with this elegant collection.

Macmillan Collector's Library: own, collect, and treasure

Discover the full range at
macmillancollectorslibrary.com

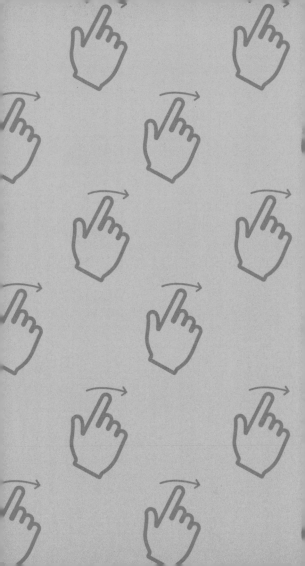